Dare County
A Brief History

David Stick

FOREWORD

Since it launched its county history series in 1963, the Historical Publications Section has published fourteen brief county histories. Over the years, one of the most popular of those titles has been David Stick's *Dare County: A Brief History,* which first appeared in 1970 and has been reprinted three times. The booklet sold out in 1991 and because of budgetary restraints remained out of print.

Now the Historical Publications Section is again pleased to make *Dare County* available to the public. The author, David Stick, the foremost historian of the Outer Banks, has enjoyed a long and distinguished career. His well-known books about the coast of North Carolina have delighted and informed many tourists and native Tar Heels alike. In *Dare County* he recounts such exciting events as the settlement of the Lost Colony on Roanoke Island, the establishment and development of lighthouses, the daring exploits of U.S. lifesavers, and the famous flight of the Wright brothers.

The Historical Publications Section also publishes Stick's *North Carolina Lighthouses,* another title popular with enthusiasts of coastal history and lore.

Joe A. Mobley
Acting Administrator
Historical Publications Section

October 1995

INTRODUCTION

The area known today as Dare County is a land of paradox and contradiction.

The first English attempt at colonization in this hemisphere was made within its present boundaries in the 1580s—yet Dare County was not formed until 1870.

Contained within its borders is an area nearly as large as the state of Rhode Island—yet it is one of North Carolina's smallest counties in terms of land area.

Its population in winter is only 6,000—yet at times in summer as many as 40,000 people live there.

It is the easternmost county in the state—yet it contains higher elevations within half a mile of the ocean than are found in some other counties far inland.

It is a land of sea and sounds, of soft breezes and hurricanes, of shipwrecks, pirates, history, and sand—mostly sand. Its story is the story of the beginning of America, the beginning of North Carolina, the beginning of the age of flight. For the person who has never been here—or has, and is inquisitive as to how it got this way—here in brief form is the story of Dare County.

David Stick

Colington Island, 1969

CONTENTS

ILLUSTRATIONS

Helicopters hover over the Wright Memorial at Kitty Hawk, the birthplace of modern aviation.

The Roanoke Colonies

In 1587, twenty years before John Smith and his associates reached Jamestown and thirty-three years before the Pilgrims landed at Plymouth Rock, a colony of 112 English men, women, and children settled on Roanoke Island in what is now Dare County. Their goal was to establish the first permanent English colony in the new world.

There had been extensive preparations for the venture in the more than three years since 1584 when Walter Raleigh was authorized by Queen Elizabeth to explore and take possession of the area north of Spanish Florida, and before 1587 more than a thousand Englishmen had already visited what is now the Dare coast.

Raleigh's first expedition, sent out in 1584, consisted of two vessels under the command of Captains Philip Amadas and Arthur Barlowe. They left England in late April, reached the Outer Banks in July, named the new land Virginia, and picked Roanoke Island as the possible site for a future settlement. Amadas and Barlowe gave a glowing account of the land and of the friendly native Indians they encountered, and when they returned to England they took with them two young Indian men, Manteo and Wanchese.

Sir Richard Grenville was in charge of Raleigh's second expedition, which was sent out in the spring of 1585. This consisted of a flotilla of seven vessels and some six hundred men, of which approximately half were soldiers. The two Indians, Manteo and Wanchese, accompanied Grenville, who explored the surrounding area before departing for England in late August leaving 107 men on Roanoke Island to build houses and a fort.

A soldier, Ralph Lane, commanded the detachment which remained on Roanoke Island through the winter of 1585-1586. He spent considerable time searching for gold in the sounds and rivers to the west, depending to a large degree on the native Indians to provide food. Despite their friendliness Lane considered the Indians savages and barbarians and treated them in a high-handed manner, culminating in a surprise attack on an Indian village in which a Roanoke chief and several other Indians were killed. From then on the Roanoke Indians refused to give further help to the Englishmen and by spring Lane's forces were suffering from an acute shortage of food.

 He fea coafts of Virginia arre full of Ilãds, wehr by the entrance into the mayne lãd
is hard to finde. For although they bee feparated with diuers and fundrie large Diui-
fion, which feeme to yeeld conuenient entrance, yet to our great perill we proued
that they wear fhallowe, and full of dangerous flatts, and could neuer perce opp
into the mayne lãd, vntill wee made trialls in many places with or fmall pinneff. At
lengthe wee fownd an entrance vppon our mens diligent ferche therof. Affter that
wee had paffed opp, and fayled ther in for afhort fpace we difcouered a migthye riuer fallnige downe
in to the fownde ouer againft thofe Ilands, which neuertheless wee could not faile opp any thinge far
by Reafon of the fhallewnes, the mouth ther of beinge annoyed with fands driuen in with the tyde
therfore faylinge further, wee came vnto a Good bigg yland, the Inhabitante therof as foone as they
faw vs began to make a great an horrible crye, as people which meuer befoer had feene men appa-
relled like vs, and camme a way makinge out crys like wild beafts or men out of their wyts. But been-
ge gentlye called backe, wee offred the of our wares, as glaffes, kniues, babies, and other trifles, which
wee thougt they deligted in. Soe they ftood ftill, and perceuinge our Good will and courtefie came
fawninge vppon vs, and bade us welcome. Then they brougt vs to their village in the iland called,
Roanoac, and vnto their Weroans or Prince, which entertained vs with Reafonable curtefie, alt-
houg the wear amafed at the firft fight of vs. Suche was our arriuall into the parte of the world,
which wee call Virginia, the flature of bodee of wich people, theyr attire, and maneer of
lyuinge, their feafts, and banketts, I will particullerlye declare vnto yow.

This engraving by Theodore DeBry is copied from a circa 1590 map by
John White of the area of the early English settlements in America. Reprinted from *The American Drawings of John White, 1577-1590*, by courtesy
of the British Museum.

In June Sir Francis Drake, having carried out successful raids against the Spaniards in Florida and the Caribbean, visited Roanoke Island on his return to England, and on learning the plight of Lane's forces offered to leave them supplies and a small vessel. While anchored off the coast, however, Drake's fleet was scattered by a storm, and Lane decided to abandon the settlement and return to England with Drake.

Had Lane remained on Roanoke Island only a week or so longer the entire course of our history might have been different, for a relief vessel sent out with supplies by Raleigh was even then approaching the coast; and within three weeks another fleet commanded by Grenville, this one consisting of three vessels, also arrived at Roanoke Island.

On finding the settlement abandoned Raleigh's relief vessel immediately returned to England, but when Grenville arrived he decided to leave fifteen men to hold the fort during the winter of 1586-1587.

Back in England that winter Raleigh, Grenville, and others who had invested in the venture made extensive preparations for turning the Roanoke Island base into a permanent settlement. The key to this was to have families settle there, and when a fleet of three vessels left England in early May, 1587, there were women and children as well as men on board.

John White, who had been to Roanoke at least once before and had made a series of watercolor paintings of what he had seen there, was in charge of this 1587 colony. Arriving at Roanoke Island in late July they found the fort demolished and no trace of the fifteen men left the previous summer by Grenville. Later they were told by the friendly Croatoan Indians that the men left by Grenville had been attacked and killed by the Roanoke tribe.

White's settlers began rebuilding the fort and repairing the houses in the "Cittie of Ralegh" and in late summer White made plans to return again to England for supplies and additional colonists. Before White departed, the friendly Indian, Manteo, was baptized; and on August 18 White's daughter, Eleanor Dare, gave birth to a child, Virginia Dare, the first child born of English parents in America. When White left Roanoke in late August his daughter and new grandchild were among the 112 men, women, and children who remained in the new world.

The plan was for White to return again in the spring of 1588, but by then England was at war with Spain and the small vessels

Two of John White's water-colors of the life of the Indians in the Roanoke Island area show an Indian man and woman eating and the Indians' manner of fishing. Reprinted from *The American Drawings of John White, 1577-1590,* by courtesy of the British Museum.

in which White left England were soon captured by the Spaniards. White was released, but because of the need for all available ships to fight the Spaniards the concerned grandfather was unable to leave again for Roanoke until March of 1590, and even then he was little more than a passenger in a fleet of three vessels commanded by Captain John Watts, who was more interested in privateering raids against the Spaniards than in relieving the colony on Roanoke Island. Thus it was August before they reached the Outer Banks, and when White went ashore he found the fort and houses deserted and no sign of the colony except the word "Croatoan" carved on a tree near the stockade.

It had been three years since White had left his settlers, and he assumed that the carved message meant that they had left Roanoke Island and had joined the Croatoan Indians near Cape Hatteras. But Captain Watts would not take time to explore further, and John White, distraught parent and grandfather, was forced to return to England without having the opportunity to search for his colony.

This was the end of the attempt at settlement on Roanoke Island, and to this day the 112 men, women, and children who disappeared there are known as the Lost Colony.

Sidelights on the Lost Colony

There has been much speculation as to what happened to the Lost Colony of Roanoke.

One prominent historian suggests that they finally gave up hope for relief from England, built a small vessel on Roanoke Island, and attempted to sail it across the Atlantic, only to be lost at sea. Others have contended that they were killed by the Spaniards, but recent research in the Spanish archives has shown that, although the Spaniards did keep a close check on the Roanoke colonists, they did not attack them.

Still another theory is that they were attacked and killed by the Roanoke Indians who had been so badly misused by Lane, but White apparently found no evidence of this, and almost certainly had such a massacre occurred the colonists could not have carved their message on the tree.

During the past quarter of a century more research has been undertaken by able historians in connection with the Roanoke settlement and the disappearance of the Lost Colony than was undertaken in the more than three hundred years after the failure of the colonization attempt, and the leading authorities have now reached some basic agreements in their conclusions.

They agree, first, that some of the lost colonists almost certainly were still alive and living with the Indians when the Jamestown colonists arrived in the Chesapeake Bay area twenty years after White left Roanoke Island in 1587. John Smith made attempts to locate or make contact with the lost colonists after hearing stories from Indians that some of them were still alive, but his efforts were fruitless.

There is a tradition among the Pembroke Indians, still living in Robeson County in southeast North Carolina, that they are descended from the Lost Colony of Roanoke. A similar tradition has been reported by the Haliwar Indians, who live near the present Carolina-Virginia border in the present-day Halifax and Warren counties. Whether or not either of these traditions is based on fact, there is every indication that some or all of the colonists abandoned their settlement on Roanoke Island and, as the tree message implied, moved to Croatoan, the present Hatteras Island. This is the conclusion offered in Paul Green's symphonic drama, *The Lost Colony,* which is presented each summer in the Waterside Theater on Roanoke Island, and it is borne out initially by White's statements and is further substantiated by traditions recounted by John Lawson in his *History of Carolina* written shortly after 1700 and by more recent archaeological explorations.

There is yet another mystery concerned with the Roanoke colonies, and this is the fact that until comparatively recently little mention was made by historians of these extensive early English colonization attempts, with the result that every child studying American history has learned of John Smith, Pocahontas, and Jamestown, and of the *Mayflower,* the Pilgrims, and Plymouth Rock, but few know anything about the earlier and extensive colony which was established in what is now Dare County, North Carolina.

One basic reason for this oversight is confusion in names. For the Roanoke colonists gave the name "Virginia" to the area surrounding Albemarle and Pamlico sounds, which they explored, as well as to all other areas north of Spanish Florida. It was nearly a hundred years before that section of the original Virginia of which Roanoke Island and Dare County are now a part became the separate colony of Carolina. To this day, when they read of the colonization attempts in "Virginia" in the 1580s most people, including some historians, do not realize that this all took place in what is now North Carolina.

The second reason, of course, is that the Roanoke colonies failed, whereas Jamestown and Plymouth Rock were successful. It is not a trait of Americans to brag about their failures.

A final sidelight on the Roanoke colonies, often overlooked, is the magnitude of the venture and its effect on future colonization attempts. In addition to producing the first accurate paintings of the New World and the first accurate maps of the east coast of North America, both by John White, the efforts resulted in detailed accounts of many of the voyages by the captains or other participants and in the first accurate description of the New World in a book by Thomas Hariot, a member of the Lane expedition, entitled *A Briefe and True Report of the New Found Land of Virginia*. These writings were widely distributed and aroused great interest throughout England in the prospects of establishing British colonies here. At the same time they provided valuable information on the land and on problems which future settlers might anticipate.

As for the magnitude of the venture, a simple listing of the voyages undertaken during the 1580s offers impressive evidence of the scope of the efforts:

1584 Amadas and Barlowe left England April 27 in two barks, reached the Outer Banks in July, explored the sounds, and returned to England in mid-September.

1585 A fleet of at least seven vessels, including a "great ship" of between 160 and 200 tons with a crew of 100 to 200 men, left Plymouth May 19, reached the Outer Banks June 26, and remained in Virginia until August 25, returning to England October 6.

1586 Sir Francis Drake's fleet of twenty-three ships anchored off the Outer Banks in June and transported Lane's colony back to England.

1586 Raleigh's relief vessel, a ship of 100 tons, reached Roanoke Island in June only to find that Lane had departed.

1586 Grenville, with three ships, arrived on the coast in late June or early July and left fifteen men on Roanoke Island.

1587 White reached Roanoke Island in July with three ships and left for the return trip to England in August.

1588 White sailed for Roanoke in two ships, but was captured by the Spaniards.

1590 Captain John Watts's fleet of three vessels, with John White as a passenger, left England in March, reached the Outer Banks in August, spent only a few hours looking for the Lost Colony, and returned to England.

Thus, between the exploratory voyage of Amadas and Barlowe in 1584 and White's fruitless effort to locate the colonists six years later, at least forty-two English vessels made the voyage to our coast.

The Province of Carolina

The Outer Banks, and in fact most of what is now North Carolina, remained part of Virginia from 1584 until King Charles II issued the Carolina Charter in 1663.

During this period of nearly eighty years English attempts to colonize Virginia continued. Once a permanent base was established at Jamestown in 1607, however, it was only natural that most of the people coming to Virginia decided to settle in that area, with its deep water access through Chesapeake Bay, and soon there were prosperous plantations along the shores of many of the tributaries of the Chesapeake.

Meanwhile other settlements were being established north of Virginia—first at Plymouth Rock in Massachusetts and later at

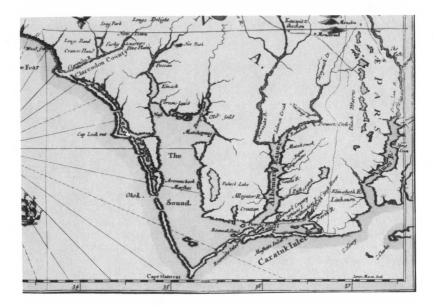

This section of the First Lords Proprietors' Map of Carolina, circa 1672, details the Outer Banks area of North Carolina. An original copy of the map is found in *Ogilby's America*.

Rhode Island, New York, Pennsylvania, New Jersey, Delaware, and Maryland.

Periodic attempts were made to colonize areas to the south, primarily in the vicinity of the Cape Fear River and of Albemarle Sound, but these efforts were unsuccessful. Consequently the permanent settlement of that part of the original Virginia which is now in North Carolina did not come until most of the best land in the vicinity of Chesapeake Bay had been claimed by plantation owners, with the result that newly arrived settlers had to go further south, or west, to find open areas in which to make their homes.

It was at this point that King Charles decided to form a new province out of the land south of the settled part of Virginia and to let eight prominent friends and businessmen share in financing the colonization of this largely unexplored territory and share also in any profits which might result from their efforts.

He named the new province Carolina and designated the eight men as the Lords Proprietors of Carolina. By terms of the Carolina Charter he issued in 1663, King Charles authorized them to colonize a vast area bounded on the south by Spanish Florida, on the north by the settled area of Virginia, on the east by the Atlantic Ocean, and on the west by the western seas. It contained all or part of thirteen present-day states.

One of the first actions taken by the Lords Proprietors in 1663 after receiving the charter was to issue a grant to one of their number, Sir John Colleton, for "the island heretofore called Carlyle now Colleton Island, lyeing near the mouth of the Chowane now Albemarle river."

Colleton proceeded immediately with plans to colonize his island, now known as Colington, and in 1664 he sent out a Captain John Whittie to establish a plantation. This was the first proprietary settlement in Carolina, and though efforts were made over a period of the next six or seven years under the direction of Peter Carteret to plant vineyards, cornfields, and tobacco and to raise cattle and hogs, a succession of severe storms ruined the crops and buildings and the project was abandoned.

Even before the failure of Carteret's Colington venture, the governor of Carolina, Samuel Stephens, received a grant to nearby Roanoke Island in 1669 and began raising cattle where eighty years earlier the Lost Colony had abandoned its fort and "cittie."

In those earliest days of Carolina settlement the main port of entry to the Albemarle Sound area, and thus to northern Carolina, was Roanoke Inlet, which was a narrow and unstable cut through the Outer Banks opposite Roanoke Island. Because vessels bound to and from the Albemarle had to pass through this inlet, the Lords Proprietors ordered their Carolina representatives in 1676 to build the "chiefe towne" of the colony on nearby Roanoke Island; apparently, though, no effort was made to carry out this order.

Despite the failure to establish a plantation on Colington Island in the 1660s or to set up a capital for the province on Roanoke Island in the 1670s, traffic through Roanoke Inlet continued to increase, and the first permanent settlers began moving into the Outer Banks area well before 1700.

These earliest permanent residents of the coastal islands were a diverse lot. Many were stockmen attracted there because the islands, surrounded as they were by water, required no fencing to contain the cattle, hogs, and sheep. Others were pilots or boatmen whose services were needed in guiding vessels through the inlets and sounds with their ever-shifting channels and shoals. Still others were individuals who, for good reason or bad, preferred to be in a locality where they could live in isolation.

In some few instances the islands were owned by the people who established homesteads there. In many others, ownership was in the hands of more well-to-do nonresidents who hired people to tend their stock, and some of these absentee owners were little more than real estate speculators. Title to Roanoke Island, for example, passed to Governor Stephens's widow at the time of his death in 1670 and then to Sir William Berkeley, governor of Virginia and one of the Lords Proprietors, whom widow Stephens married. The Berkeleys sold the island for 100 pounds to a New England merchant named Joshua Lamb in 1676; and Lamb turned a quick profit by selling a one half interest to Nicholas Paige of Boston for 150 pounds a year later and then selling a quarter of the island to George Patridge.

Another important factor which influenced the early settlement of the Outer Banks, and which was of considerable concern to the Lords Proprietors, was the large number of ships being wrecked on the coast and the equally large number of dead whales drifting ashore there. In 1678 they appointed Robert Houlden to take possession in their name of "all wrecks, ambergrice or other ejections of sea," and John Lawson reported about 1700 that the extraction of oil and whalebone from dead whales was the primary occupation of a group of Carolinians "that inhabit the Banks and Sea-Side, where they dwell for that Intent, and for the Benefit of Wrecks, which sometimes fall in upon the Shoar."

There was also proprietary concern that people suspected of being pirates or runaway slaves were seeking refuge on the banks, and when the British frigate H.M.S. *Hady* was driven ashore on the north banks in 1696 there was a report that the bankers "got some of her guns ashore and shot into her sides and disabled her from getting off" so that they could steal her cargo.

Thus by 1700 stockmen, whalers, wreckers, pilots, and possibly runaways and pirates were living on the Outer Banks, and the permanent settlement of what is now Dare County had finally begun.

The Colonial Period

Regardless of where a person may live there is a growing awareness of his need for a reliable source of water. On the Outer Banks this need is magnified many times, for water has been the key factor in shaping the history of the area and the lives of its residents from the moment the first of Raleigh's colonists sighted its dim silhouette in the distance until yesterday afternoon when yet another tourist crossed one of the modern bridges connecting with the mainland and found himself at sea.

The Outer Banks, of which Dare County is an integral part, is a string of low, narrow islands jutting out into the Atlantic, protecting the mainland from the ravages of the sea, yet at the same time obstructing the passage of oceangoing vessels to inland ports.

Often the nearby waters appear placid, yet even when the surface is calm there is turmoil in the depths below. Three basic counteracting forces are constantly at work on the sea side of these islands. The first is the force of ocean waves, often fetching across hundreds of miles of open sea to break with fury on the shore. The second is the Gulf Stream, the "ocean river," a vast body of warm water moving steadily northward, caressing the tip of Diamond Shoals off Cape Hatteras before passing into the North Atlantic. The third is the littoral drift along this coast, a steady flow near the shore of cold waters stemming from the Labrador Current, carrying sediment and debris with it and always moving to the south.

Yet another constant force, this one from the sound side of the islands, adds to the turmoil beneath the surface. This one begins in the mountains of Virginia and North Carolina where rains fall and trickle into gullies and streams to form rivers which flow ever eastward, through the broad sounds in their search for outlets to the sea. Billions of gallons of water pass yearly in this manner through the openings in the Outer Banks to collide with the ocean waves or littoral drift or the Gulf Stream. And though the openings formed are called inlets, they are in fact outlets.

So powerful are these forces of water that they are constantly reshaping the sandy shores of the Outer Banks and the channels and shoals adajacent to them. Inevitably they also shape the lives of the human beings who choose to live there.

At no time in history has the water affected the course of events on these islands more dramatically than during the formative three-quarters of a century between 1700 and the outbreak of the Revolution in 1775—the colonial period in Outer Banks history.

There was a compelling need then, as there is today, for a safe and stable channel connecting Albemarle Sound with the sea. In the 1580s the Raleigh colonists came to depend on Port Ferdinando, opposite the southern end of Roanoke Island, for passage from sea to sound. In the 1660s Captain Whittie and those who followed him used Roanoke Inlet, ten or twelve miles to the north, which was reported to have a depth of between eleven and fifteen feet over the bar. But by the early 1700s Roanoke Inlet had begun to shoal badly and it was difficult to find even a ten-foot channel.

Though the people did not know it at the time, nature was playing one of its subtle pranks by gradually diverting the flow of river water from the east to the west of Roanoke Island. The result was that, instead of passing out to sea through Roanoke Inlet, more and more water was flowing into Pamlico Sound and then through Ocracoke Inlet to the Atlantic. Since the steady flow of water is what keeps these inlets open, the devastating effect of this change in currents was the eventual closing of Roanoke Inlet, and by the 1730s there was no direct, reliable outlet through the banks from the Roanoke Island area and Roanoke Sound.

Two abortive attempts were made to establish port towns on Roanoke Island, in one of which the town was officially established and named Carteret, but there was no need for a port town opposite an inlet which vessels could not use and both efforts failed.

Stockmen continued to use the islands, and more and more settlers seeking seclusion and opportunity adjacent to the sea received grants for land on the banks and moved there. Whales continued to wash up on the shore, sailing vessels continued to wreck on the shoals, and finally in 1718 the rumors of piracy became fact.

In the spring of 1718 a Captain Drummond appeared on the Outer Banks with a fleet of four vessels and nearly four hundred men. He used the name Edward Teach, or Thatch, but those aware of his past knew him as the infamous pirate Blackbeard. The pirate soon disposed of two of his vessels and most of his men, disclaimed all further intent to go a-pirating, and received a royal pardon from Governor Charles Eden of North Carolina.

Making his headquarters at Bath and Ocracoke, but sailing far afield, Blackbeard showed up at one point with a French vessel loaded with sugar and cocoa which he claimed he had discovered abandoned at sea. There began then a period of terror for residents of the coast, for Blackbeard seemed to delight in attacking and molesting almost everyone with whom he came in contact, even small vessels in the sounds.

Appeals were made to Governor Eden for help, but there were well-founded rumors that the governor was sharing in the pirate's booty, and eventually the North Carolinians turned to Governor Alexander Spottswood of Virginia, who sent two small sloops to the Outer Banks in search of Blackbeard. They found him at Ocracoke, and after a brief but fierce battle in which Blackbeard's vessel, the *Adventure*, and both British vessels were disabled, Blackbeard was killed and most of his crew captured.

Regularly, still, people search the Outer Banks for Blackbeard's treasure, but so far as is known none of it has been discovered. Possibly the reason can be found in a statement Blackbeard is said to have made shortly before his death when he was asked where his treasure was hidden. The pirate reportedly replied that "nobody but himself and the Devil knew where it was—and the longest liver should take it all."

Even as organized piracy was being wiped out the native

Indians were suffering a similar fate. In desperation the mainland Indians, probably remnants of the Roanoke tribe, attacked the settlers on Roanoke Island and across the sounds in 1711 and again in 1713, killing or carrying off more than forty white people.

In retaliatory attacks by the white settlers most of the warring Indians were wiped out, and the only natives still living on the Outer Banks were a handful of friendly Indians on Hatteras Island, no doubt descendents of the Croatoans who had befriended the Raleigh colonists. But disease and poverty and the alien society of the white settlers gradually took their toll there too, and by the end of the colonial period the native Indians had been exterminated.

The Revolution

There were no Revolutionary War battles on the Outer Banks, no devastation by invading armies, not even naval warfare in the context of fleet against fleet. But the war came early to the coast and continued to the very end, for the Outer Banks stockmen had an abundance of the one commodity the British needed most—fresh meat.

The British foraging raids were most often carried out by small armed vessels or tenders, and they became so numerous by the spring of 1776 that the North Carolina Provincial Congress sent a special committee to the banks for a firsthand investigation.

The committee reported that the coastal islands were "covered with cattle, sheep and hogs" and "the few inhabitants living on the banks are chiefly persons whose estates consist in live stock." They found the Outer Banks defenseless and "exposed to the ravages" of the British and recommended that immediate defensive measures be taken.

"If the armed vessels and tenders are prevented from getting supplies of fresh provisions from the sea coast," the committee reported, "it will be impossible for the war to be of long continuance in this Province, as the seamen and soldiers will be afflicted with the scurvy and other diseases, arising from the constant use of salt provisions, and therefore be under the necessity of quitting the coast."

They concluded that the best way to accomplish this was to sign up recruits in the coastal area and form them into independent companies to receive the same pay as troops in the continental army. Ten days later the Provincial Congress authorized five such units and named Dennis Dauge as captain of the company which was to be responsible for protecting the coast between Currituck Inlet and Roanoke Inlet. Serving under Dauge were John Jarvis as first lieutenant, Legrand Whitehall as second lieutenant, and Butler Cowall as ensign, plus four sergeants, four corporals, two drummers, one fifer, and sixty-eight rank and file.

Unfortunately, the money ran out and it became necessary to disband the coastal defense units, thus leaving it up to the individual bankers to repel the British foraging raids. To make matters worse, able-bodied men from the coast were being drafted for service elsewhere, and in November, 1778, Representative Samuel Jarvis of Currituck County appealed to Governor Richard Caswell to let the banks men remain at home, since the enemy was "constantly landing men and plundering."

Typical of the raids was one reported in the summer of 1779 by W. Russell, commander of the Hyde militia which then served on Hatteras Island. Five British vessels, including two brigs, a schooner, a sloop, and a small boat, he said "came to anchor a little to the Northward of Cape Hatteras" and "seeing a gang of cattle near the shore" sent three boats ashore. However, the vessels had been spotted by local residents who "were concealed amongst the Hills," and as soon as the British left their boats and started after the cattle the bankers "rushed down upon them, killed five and took their muskets and several other articles they left behind."

In addition to these landing parties seeking livestock, the British also sent small privateers on raids against coastal shipping, particularly in the vicinity of the inlets. Especially active in these raids were two captains who had operated on the coast before the war, Captain John Goodrich and Captain John McLean, both of whom were reported by the *North Carolina Gazette* (New Bern) in its issue of July 17, 1778, as "having lately cut several vessels and small craft out of Roanoke and Currituck Inlets."

One of the vessels mentioned in this account was a small schooner owned by a man named Etheridge, which McLean refitted and made into a privateer. But these raids were not all one-sided, for when Captain McLean sent the refitted Etheridge vessel back to the north banks for still another raid, the bankers recaptured her.

Ships continued to wreck on the coast, and since most of the vessels operating off the Outer Banks were British, their losses were particularly heavy. In the space of a few months during early 1779 two vessels of the British fleet, the ship *Tartar* and the brigantine *Surprise,* came ashore on the north banks, and in both instances the militia under command of Samuel Jarvis took possession of the vessels and captured all members of their crews—seventy officers and men from the *Tartar* and thirty from the *Surprise.*

By the end of the war a visitor would have seen few changes on the Outer Banks. Despite the repeated raids on livestock by the British there was no noticeable reduction in the quantity of cattle, sheep, and hogs running loose on the islands, and shipwrecks continued to provide both excitement and a source of income. Whether in peace or war, as part of a British colony or as one of the thirteen new United States, the Outer Banks was still a string of isolated islands separated from the mainland by broad sounds and subjected to the ravages of sea and wind.

Early Life on the Outer Banks

The recorded history of what is now North Carolina's Dare County covers a span of nearly four centuries, but for simplification it can be divided easily into three distinct periods.

The first is the era of exploration, colonization, and initial settlement, beginning with the Raleigh colonies and continuing to the end of the Revolution, in all nearly two hundred years.

The last is a period of tremendous change, still being witnessed, which began with the construction of the first bridges linking the islands with the mainland only forty years ago.

In between is a span of nearly a century and a half during which there evolved on the Outer Banks a distinctive pattern of life and activity, of speech and dress and habit.

Land ownership was the key to the beginning of this new era in the 1780s. For until then, under British colonial status, a large portion of the land on the Outer Banks had been owned by a relatively small number of wealthy people. Most of these were nonresidents, and many of them had never even visited their property. On the other hand a large number of the people living on the coastal islands did not own the land on which they resided and therefore were simply squatters.

Independence changed this—independence, and the creation

of a government by the people and for the people. Land previously owned by the British government or its agents now became state property, and any citizen of North Carolina could apply for a grant for a portion of these state lands. In addition many large property owners now found it both profitable and expedient to sell small parcels to people who had already settled there or planned to move to the coastal islands, since such a person could establish title anyway by what was known as squatter's rights.

During the first six years after the end of the war sixty-two deeds were filed in the Currituck courthouse for land on the north banks, including nine on Colington and thirty-one at Kitty Hawk and nearby Jeanguite.

By that time most of the residents of Roanoke Island listed their occupation as farmer or planter, while those on Hatteras Island and the north banks referred to themselves for the most part as stockmen or mariners. But regardless of what a man chose to call himself it was necessary for him to develop a high degree of self-sufficiency in order to survive on the coast, since every man had to master at least a modicum of the skill of the mariner, farmer, stockman, carpenter, boat builder, fisherman, and hunter.

Because of continued dependence on water transportation within the area and increased traffic in nearby coastal shipping, the new governments of the state and union became concerned early with the problems of navigation. Numerous acts were passed by the fledgling General Assembly of the state to provide for marking channels with buoys and other navigational aids, and as early as 1787 the assembly authorized the incorporation of the Raleigh Canal Company to construct an artificial inlet from Roanoke Island to the sea in the vicinity of Nags Head so that there would be direct access from the Albemarle to the ocean. This project failed, as did numerous others proposed for the same purpose in the years which followed.

Providing navigational aids for vessels at sea became a federal responsibility, and in 1794 Congress authorized construction of a lighthouse "on the headlands of Cape Hatteras." Built of natural sandstone the structure was not completed until 1802, and even then its beacon was not normally visable on the outer reaches of Diamond Shoals. An effort was then made to place buoys on the shoals, but these soon washed away, and in 1825 a specially designed lightship, completed at a cost of $25,000, was anchored off the outer tip of Diamond Shoals. Two years

Cape Hatteras lighthouse, as it appears today, still stands sentinel at Diamond Shoals. Photograph by Aycock Brown, Manteo.

later, however, it broke loose in a hurricane and was wrecked near Ocracoke.

The increased numbers of shipwrecks, and problems concerned with the ownership of wrecked vessels and cargoes, brought early state action in dividing the entire coast into wreck districts with a state agent in each whose assignment was to take possession of anything which washed up on the beach, determine rightful ownership, and when necessary conduct public auctions. This type of auction was known as a vendue, and the man in charge was a vendue master or wreck commissioner.

Government action in placing lighthouses, lightships, and buoys in the area as aids to navigation and in establishing wreck districts and naming vendue masters to dispose of wrecks and cargo still did not involve government in the important task of trying to save the lives of shipwrecked mariners, and practically everyone on the banks automatically became a volunteer lifesaver when such services were needed. To organize this important work the state in 1801 charged vendue masters with the responsibility of rounding up residents to assist him in giving aid to any vessel which was wrecked or in danger of being wrecked on the coast.

The unusual conditions on the Outer Banks and the peculiar needs of the residents resulted in their designing distinctive structures especially suited to their needs. A type of two-story house, one room deep, with a breezeway and detached kitchen in back soon evolved, and as early as 1806 a visitor named William Tatham was impressed with the "two story houses, and comfortable living" in the community nestled in the woods behind Cape Hatteras.

Almost every resident was engaged in fishing as a means of

18

providing food for his table, and some made a business of it, usually trading their fish catch on the mainland for provisions and corn. This brought on the need for mills on the coast, and a special type of windmill evolved, the whole structure being mounted on a central axis so that it could be rotated and the sails set to catch the prevailing winds. These windmills were located in every community and became so numerous that one visitor stated "there are a greater number than I supposed were in existence in the whole country."

A profusion of oak and cedar in the forests on the sound side of the islands spawned an extensive shipbuilding industry, and the village of Kinnakeet, now Avon, at one time was the center of this activity. Again the needs of the area and the ingenuity of the residents resulted in the development of a special type of sailboat, later known as a Pamlico Sound fisherman, or shad boat, which was especially adapted for use in the shallow sounds.

Storms and hurricanes continued to be a factor in life on the banks, though most people built their homes in wooded "ham-

This is a windmill of the type used by the inhabitants of the Outer Banks during the nineteenth century. Photograph from Jerry Schumacher, Morehead City.

A shad boat, developed for use in the shallow waters along the Outer Banks, sails on Albemarle Sound around 1885. Photograph by Ralph M. Monroe, loaned by H. I. Chapelle.

mocks" on the soundside where they had protection from high winds and flood waters. One notable hurricane in September, 1846, opened two new inlets on the banks, one just south of Roanoke Island and the other between Hatteras and Ocracoke, and these two—Oregon Inlet and Hatteras Inlet—remain today as the major inlets on the Dare coast.

Though the first federal census was taken in 1790, it was not until the census of 1850 that the head count was conducted in such a manner as to pinpoint the population in each of the coastal islands. By then there were approximately 400 families in what is now Dare County, including nearly 2,500 people, of whom approximately 280 were slaves. More than half the slaves were on Roanoke Island, which had a total population of 610. Other census figures showed 661 people, including 104 slaves, in the Cape Hatteras area; 318 residents of Kinnakeet; 206 people living at Chicamacomico; and 576, including 30 slaves, on the north banks.

Thus, on the eve of the Civil War the pattern of life on the Outer Banks had taken its distinctive shape.

The Civil War

Soon after the outbreak of the Civil War it became apparent to the leadership on both sides that control of the Outer Banks and of the sound waters behind them was a key to the control of all of northeastern North Carolina.

By this time Hatteras Inlet, which had been open only fifteen years, was the deepest and most stable channel through the banks, and the Confederates soon began work on two fortifications, Fort Hatteras and Fort Clark, for its defense. Located

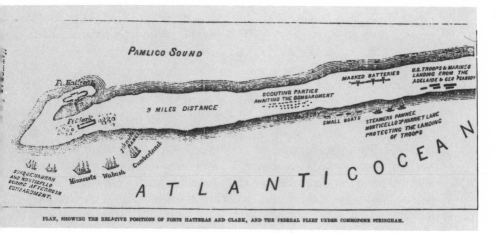

PAMLICO SOUND

Fr. Hatteras

3 MILES DISTANCE

Ft. Clark

Minnesota Wabash Cumberland

SUSQUEHANNAH
AND MONTICELLO
DURING AFTERNOON
BOMBARDMENT.

MASKED BATTERIES

SCOUTING PARTIES
AWAITING THE BOMBARDMENT

SMALL BOATS

STEAMERS PAWNEE
MONTICELLO 2ª HARRIET LANE
PROTECTING THE LANDING
OF TROOPS

U.S. TROOPS & MARINES
LANDING FROM THE
ADELAIDE & GEO PEABODY

A T L A N T I C   O C E A N

PLAN, SHOWING THE RELATIVE POSITIONS OF FORTS HATTERAS AND CLARK, AND THE FEDERAL FLEET UNDER COMMODORE STRINGHAM.

A drawing from *Frank Leslie's Illustrated Newspaper,* September 7, 1861, shows the positions of Forts Hatteras and Clark on Hatteras Island and the federal fleet under Commodore Stringham.

on the Cape Hatteras side of the inlet, the forts were built of sand sheathed with two-inch planks and covered with a protective layer of marsh grass and turf.

At Oregon Inlet, the only other navigable inlet on the northern coast, construction was started on a similar but smaller installation named Fort Oregon, which was located on the south side of that inlet.

Even as the work progressed on these shore defenses the side-wheel steamer *Winslow,* flagship of the fledgling North Carolina navy, began preying on enemy coastal shipping from its Hatteras Inlet base and soon ran up an amazing record of capturing at least sixteen Union prizes, including a bark, three brigs, and several schooners loaded with valuable cargo.

In Washington at this point there was more concern over putting a stop to the privateering raids of the *Winslow* and in halting the flow of Confederate supplies through Hatteras Inlet than there was in gaining control of the Outer Banks, but the only way to stop the raids was to capture Forts Hatteras and Clark.

Accordingly, in late August of 1861, a joint naval and ground attack was launched against the Hatteras Inlet defenses with a fleet of seven vessels and a landing force of approximately one thousand men. This Union fleet included some of the finest war-

21

ships in the service, mounting altogether a total of 143 guns, as opposed to an armament of 12 short-range guns at Fort Hatteras and 6 at Fort Clark. The Federal ground forces also had superiority, since the garrison of both forts consisted of only 580 men.

War was a new experience to most of the participants on both sides. Confederate Captain Thomas Sparrow, who arrived in the midst of the battle with reinforcements, said later that he had "never before seen a shell explode." He added, "It was sometime before I got to understand the thing. I saw from time to time beautiful little puffs of white, silvery smoke hanging over the fort without at first being able to account for them. I soon learned to know that it was where a shell had burst in the air, leaving the smoke or gas behind it, while the fragments had descended on their mission of destruction."

Despite potentially serious setbacks experienced by the Union forces, including the sinking of all the landing barges in the Hatteras surf, which resulted in loss of contact between the fleet and the troops ashore, and the grounding of two vessels in the inlet, the terrific bombardment from the attacking vessels resulted in a Union victory.

The original plan had been to sink vessels loaded with stone in the inlet in order to prevent its further use by Confederate vessels, but instead the Union forces decided to keep the inlet open and maintain control over it by stationing detachments in the captured forts.

The North Carolina troops who had escaped from Hatteras Inlet then made their way up the sound to Roanoke Island, and shortly reinforcements, including a Georgia regiment, joined them there in building new defensive works to protect the northern sounds.

In the ensuing months there was a single encounter between the Federal troops left at Hatteras to defend the captured forts and the North Carolina and Georgia forces who were building new works on Roanoke Island. This took place in early October, 1861, on the banks at Chicamacomico and began with the Confederates chasing the Union forces down the beach to Cape Hatteras one day and the Federals chasing the Southerners back up the banks the next. Neither side could claim a clear victory, and the affair became known as "the Chicamacomico Races."

The real battle was shaping up over control of Roanoke Island. In preparation for it the North Carolina and Georgia troops,

The Twentieth Indiana Regiment bivouacked at the Cape Hatteras lighthouse on October 4, 1861, after their march of twenty-five miles from Chicamacomico. Illustration from the National Archives.

later reinforced with Wise's Virginia Legion, constructed three forts on the north end of Roanoke Island overlooking Croatan Sound, sank a line of obstructions across the sound, and built smaller defensive works on a swamp-lined causeway midway the island and elsewhere on the eastern shore.

General Ambrose Burnside, in command of the Federal forces being assembled for the attack, got together one of the strangest fleets ever to engage in battle. The plan was to enlist men from the northern seacoast, primarily Massachusetts and his native Rhode Island, "many of whom would be familiar with the coasting trade" and attack Roanoke Island with a fleet of light-draft steamers, sailing vessels, and barges. Here is how General Burnside described what even he admitted was a "motley fleet":

"North River barges and propellers had been strengthened from deck to keelson by heavy oak planks, and water-tight compartments had been build in them," he said. "They were so arranged that parapets of sand-bags or bales of hay could be built

23

These contemporary engravings show the landing of troops on Roanoke Island during the Burnside Expedition in February, 1862. Photograph, top, from the North Carolina Collection, University of North Carolina; bottom, from Evert A. Duyckinck, *National History of the Late Civil War*, II, facing 249.

upon their decks, and each one carried from four to six guns. Sailing vessels, formerly belonging to the coasting trade, had been fitted up in the same manner. Several large passenger steamers, which were guaranteed to draw less than eight feet of water, together with tugs and ferry boats, served to make up the fleet."

The attack was scheduled for January, 1862, but a succession of storms made it impossible for the fleet to navigate successfully the swash at Hatteras Inlet, and for nearly a month the more than eighty vessels of the fleet remained bottled up there. When finally the last vessel crossed into the sound and the fleet headed for Roanoke Island the actual battle proved almost anticlimatic.

It began on the morning of February 10, 1862, when the Federal warships opened fire on the Roanoke Island forts, and throughout that day the action was limited to a steady exchange of fire between the two. Late that afternoon Burnside's troops began landing at Ashby's Harbor above Wanchese on the west shore of Roanoke Island.

By dawn the next morning a force of 7,500 Federal troops moved up the narrow causeway in the center of the island for a frontal attack on Fort Russell, the three-gun battery erected by the Confederates to defend the causeway. Five regiments left the main force to move against the battery through heavy swamps on the left, and five more regiments made a similar approach from the right. When these three columns reached the battery and charged, the small Confederate defensive force abandoned the fortification and retreated toward the north end of the island.

Shortly thereafter Colonel H. M. Shaw, commanding the defenders, formally surrendered the island, its forts, approximately 2,675 officers and men who had been unable to escape, and the control of the sounds of northeastern North Carolina.

Few residents of the coastal islands had been participants in these activities, and they were viewed as a strange breed by soldiers on both sides. "Apparently indifferent to this outside sphere," said one Confederate officer, "they constitute a world within themselves." Another visitor said, "Queer folks in this region! . . . Most of them were born here, never saw any other locality and all are happy."

As for allegiance, their ties through history had been as close to the North as to North Carolina, and they were accused of expressing their neutrality "by raising white flags to the housetops on the approach of either Confederates or Federals." In actual practice, however, most of the bankers took the oath of allegiance to the United States soon after the area was captured, and some even participated in forming a provisional government for the "loyal" state of North Carolina at Hatteras.

An unusual aftermath of the Federal victory at Roanoke Island was that slaves from all over the Albemarle area headed for the island as soon as they learned that it had been captured. Within a few months several thousand freed slaves were living in a hastily constructed community on the north end of the island, and with encouragement from the Freedman's Bureau each family was eligible to acquire a small plot of confiscated land and build a home. In this manner more than five hundred houses were built by the ex-slaves, thus forming near Fort Raleigh the largest community on the Outer Banks. But so many of the able-bodied men were drafted into the Federal army that the community was soon inhabited only by women and children, with most of the men who remained there being either old or crippled. Eventually the problem of caring for these people became so acute that the colony was broken up, the freed slaves were removed to other captured areas, and the lands were returned to their former owners.

The Lifesavers

After the Civil War there was a tremendous increase in the use of the shipping lanes off the Outer Banks, the bulk of it by sailing vessels. So many of these encountered trouble along our coast and ended up as shipwrecks that the Cape Hatteras area became known as "the Graveyard of the Atlantic."

For nearly a century there had been determined efforts to devise methods of warning ships away from the treacherous coast, mainly by the erection of lighthouses on shore and by placing lightships and beacons at sea. But these aids to navigation were found to be entirely inadequate.

Even less had been done in the way of assisting mariners unfortunate enough to be wrecked on the coast. Except for the authority given wreck commissioners to organize rescue parties, most of the lifesaving activities were handled by the local residents of the Outer Banks on a volunteer basis.

Finally, in the 1870s, the United States government launched a dual program to take care of these pressing problems.

The first action was to construct a series of tall lighthouses along the coast designed to have sufficient power in their beacons, and to be close enough together, so that coastal vessels could pick up the signal from the one ahead before losing sight of the last one astern.

In this manner modern brick lighthouses were constructed at Cape Hatteras, Bodie Island, and Currituck Beach. Each had distinctive colors and markings so that they could be identified easily in the daytime—Cape Hatteras lighthouse, for example, had alternate black and white spirals, while Bodie Island had alternate black and white horizontal strips and Currituck Beach was painted solid red.

For identification at night each was designed with a distinctive sequence of flashing lights, with specific intervals between the flashes.

The Cape Hatteras lighthouse, intended to be "the most imposing brick lighthouse on this continent, if not in the world"

The lifesaving station at the village of Kinnakeet, pictured here circa 1893 to 1899, was one of a string of such stations located every seven miles along the Outer Banks. Photograph from the collection of Collier Cobb, courtesy of Miss Mary Cobb, Chapel Hill.

was 180 feet high and was completed December 16, 1870. Bodie Island was 150 feet high and was put into service October 1, 1872, while Currituck Beach, also 150 feet high, was first lighted December 1, 1875.

Even as work was in progress on these three impressive structures other construction crews were erecting at intervals along the coast seven small buildings which were to be used as lifesaving stations. The first of these was put into service in 1874, and others were added in succeeding years until shortly there were lifesaving stations from one end of the Outer Banks to the other spaced approximately seven miles apart.

Originally the stations were manned only during the winter months, then a keeper was hired for permanent duty, and finally the stations were fully staffed throughout the year.

Each station was equipped with surfboats and with horses and wagons to haul the boats up and down the beach. In time a system of round-the-clock patrols was put into effect, by which a surfman from each station would walk halfway to the next station, check in at a little shack called a "halfway house" and then walk back to his own station again. In this manner, for many years, approximately every three and a half miles along the entire length of this coast there was a surfman on foot or horse patrol, day and night, 365 days each year. At the same time

A lifesaving crew, circa 1899, pulls its surfboat across the beach to aid a stranded vessel. Photograph from the National Archives.

a constant watch was also maintained in the lookout tower of each station.

The basic responsibility of the surfman on patrol was to try to spot vessels which had come too close to shore and warn them off before they were wrecked. For this purpose he carried a specially designed flare with which to signal vessels in danger, and hundreds of ships were saved in this manner.

Often, especially during storms, the surfman would discover the vessels already in the surf or grounded on sandbars offshore. At night sometimes his first awareness of trouble would be the sound of shrill voices crying for help.

Unless the wrecked vessel had already broken up, with crewmen and passengers trying to swim ashore or drifting in on wreckage, the surfman would normally rush back to his station for help. Frequently when the vessel was close enough to shore the lifesavers would fire a line over the wreck and haul the survivors to safety in what was known as a breeches buoy.

The real heroism of the lifesavers was most often demonstrated, however, in those instances when the wreck was too far offshore to be reached by a breeches buoy line, and it became necessary to try to launch a boat through the pounding surf and attempt to row out to the wrecked vessel at sea. The annals of the United States Life Saving Service, and of its successor the United States Coast Guard, are filled with official accounts of such feats.

The *Priscilla* wrecked and broke up on the Dare coast in 1899. Photograph from the collection of Collier Cobb, courtesy of Miss Mary Cobb.

Gradually, after 1900, sailing ships were being replaced by steamships, and by World War I there had been a marked decline in the number of shipwrecks. At this point the German U-boats took up the slack, and during the year 1918 no less than fifteen vessels were sunk on the coast, most of them by German submarines or mines.

The lifesaving stations continued in service throughout the 1920s and 1930s, though shipwrecks became more and more infrequent. Then, in January, 1942, with the United States again at war, the German submarines struck once more. During the next six months more than fifty vessels, a large proportion of them tankers carrying much needed supplies of gasoline and fuel for the Allied forces, were sunk off the Outer Banks by the enemy subs. The attacks were most often made at night, and there were times when the sea and sky were lighted for miles by burning oil. By the summer of 1942 the destruction of friendly shipping was largely halted by the combined efforts of newly built Coast Guard patrol planes and Navy blimps and the activities of antisubmarine vessels and extensive use of mine fields.

Following World War II airplanes and helicopters from the Coast Guard Air Base at nearby Elizabeth City took over much of the work previously handled by the shore units, and the bulk of the old lifesaving stations were taken out of service, for the most part leaving only those located close to inlets.

Despite these modern improvements in navigation and in aids to mariners, vessels still occasionally come ashore on the Outer Banks. Usually there is advance warning, though, and modern lifesaving methods and equipment can be put to work on a moment's notice. The days of the lifesavers operating on foot from the isolated shore stations are past, but their heroic deeds will never be forgotten.

The Formation of Dare County

Counties are geographical and political subdivisions of the state which have been formed by the General Assembly in order to bring government functions closer to the people.

Actually the first North Carolina counties were established long before the state was formed. This was in the early colonial period when it became obvious to the British that the necessary services of government—law enforcement, holding court, recording deeds, and collecting property taxes to pay for these services —could not be handled effectively from a central capital.

By 1700 there were five North Carolina counties, all in the vicinity of Albemarle Sound. This number had increased to thirteen counties located along the eastern seaboard by 1740, and to thirty-five extending westward to the mountains by 1775. At that time Roanoke Island and the northern coast of what is now Dare County were part of Currituck County, the southern coast including Cape Hatteras was part of Hyde County, and the western part, on the mainland, was part of Tyrrell County.

It was nearly a hundred years later, in 1870, that the General Assembly voted to take away these parts of Currituck, Hyde, and Tyrrell to form a new county. They named it Dare County in memory of Virginia Dare and established the county seat at the newly settled community of Manteo on the east side of Roanoke Island opposite Nags Head.

Many of the problems faced by the new county resulted from the fact that it consisted of relatively small land areas separated by sounds and inlets. Thus the four main sections of the new county of Dare—Cape Hatteras and the south banks, Nags Head and the north banks, Roanoke Island, and the mainland—were accessible to each other only by boat. To compound the transportation difficulties most of the mainland area was a vast swamp without roads or trails, and the four mainland communities of Stumpy Point, Manns Harbor, East Lake, and Mashoes were cut off from each other by water.

For taxing purposes the new county was divided into five townships. Two of these, Hatteras and Kinnekeet, were located on the south banks of Hatteras Island and two more, Croatan and East Lake, were located on the mainland. The fifth township, Nags Head, consisted of all of Roanoke Island as well as the north banks from Oregon Inlet to the south edge of the community of Kitty Hawk.

To govern the new county three commissioners were elected at large, as was a sheriff, a register of deeds, and a clerk of court. A new courthouse was built in the county seat, and when this burned it was replaced in 1904 by the current building, with the courtroom on the top floor of the large brick structure and the county offices on the ground floor.

When citizens came to the county seat from any of the outlying townships or from Nags Head they had to come by boat, and on court days it was not an uncommon sight to see hundreds

A fishing party docks its shad boat, which was developed in Currituck Sound, in Manteo in 1899. Photograph from the collection of Collier Cobb, courtesy of Miss Mary Cobb.

of small sailboats, many of them being the shad boats especially designed for use in the shallow sounds, tied up in Shallowbag Bay on the Manteo waterfront.

Whereas today it is possible to drive from any part of Dare County to Manteo in a little over an hour, in those early days— and in fact until the 1930s—a sailing trip to the county seat from Nags Head or Colington on the north banks, or from any of the communities on the mainland, involved at least one full day and often two; and a trip from Hatteras and the south banks just to record a deed in the courthouse was at least a two-day outing.

In North Carolina, for all practical purposes, the counties are little more than appendages of the state government, since all of the responsibility and authority of the board of county commissioners and other officials are spelled out in detail by the state constitution or by state statutes. The county governing body, the board of commissioners, does not have the authority to make laws or pass ordinances, and any changes in government operations and procedures on the county level must be approved by the General Assembly in Raleigh.

From the beginning, because the population of Dare was so small and the communities so widely separated, it was impractical if not impossible to carry out all county governmental func-

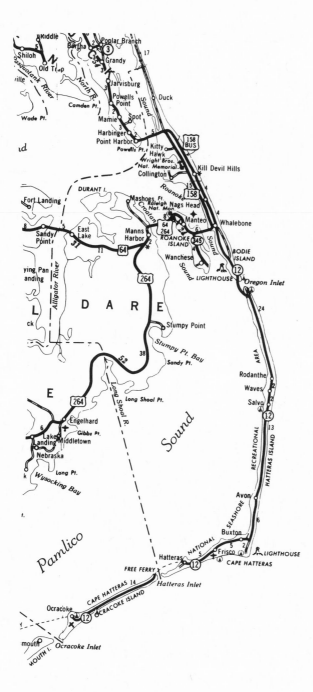

The boundaries of modern Dare County are outlined on the official North Carolina highway map.

tions in the exact manner prescribed by the state. During many lengthy periods there was no lawyer residing in the county, and at all times it was extremely difficult for county officers to travel to the state capital. For this reason different methods of conducting the county's business, which were particularly suited to the needs of this isolated area, were put into practice in Dare County. As recently as the 1940s it was frequently said that there were two ways to do things in North Carolina: either the Dare County way, or the way they were done in the other ninety-nine counties.

Not long after the establishment of the county in 1870 people living in the communities on the north banks realized that new problems had resulted from the fact that Nags Head and Colington were in Dare County, but that the adjoining banks communities of Kitty Hawk and Duck were still in Currituck. Consequently, in 1920, the General Assembly took away from Currituck the north banks area from Kitty Hawk Bay to Caffey's Inlet and added it to Dare. Subsequently a sixth township, known as Atlantic Township, was formed from this newly acquired area plus Colington Island and what is now the town of Kill Devil Hills.

Place Names and Post Offices

Many people become so accustomed to hearing the names of places around them that they eventually reach the point where they use the names automatically, without thought of how they sound, what they mean, or where they originated.

For historians, however, one of the best and most interesting ways to trace the history of an area is to determine when and why place names first appeared and how and why they were changed, and a simple way to do this is to compare the names on modern maps with those on maps made by earlier explorers and settlers.

When the Raleigh colonists came to what is now Dare County in the 1580s Captain John White prepared maps of the area, and another member of the colony named Thomas Hariot wrote an account of the colonists' experiences and travels, and in the process the colonists gave names to many places which still exist.

Nags Head was Etacrewac on the White maps, Salvo was Cape Kenrick, Manns Harbor was Dasemunkepeuc, and Cape Hatteras was Cape S. John. There was an inlet above Buxton called Chacandepeco, two others in the area of Bodie Island known as

34

Port Lane and Port Ferdinando, and a fourth in the vicinity of Southern Shores named Trinitie Harbor.

The name Hatarask (Hatteras) was used by the Raleigh colonists, but it referred to the Pea Island area; and Croatoan (Croatan) was west of Cape Hatteras. Of all the names in use in the 1580s only one, Roanoac Island (Roanoke Island), still applies to the same place.

By the time permanent settlement had begun and the province of Carolina had been established three quarters of a century after the disappearance of Raleigh's "Lost Colonists," the maps showed both Cape Hatteras and Croatan with their present-day spelling and in their present locations. Roanoke Island was then spelled Roanoake, and there was an inlet of the same name at Nags Head. Alligator River was shown and named as it is today, and an island named Carlyle was in the process of being changed to Colleton (Colington) Island.

Man's (Manns Harbor), Body I. (Bodie Island), and Chickehauk (Kitty Hawk) all appeared first on maps in the 1730s. People were living at Kinekeet (Kinnakeet) in 1774, and at the start of the Revolution in 1775 present names had been given to Wimble Shoals, Hatteras Banks, Nag's Head, Stumpy Point, Currituck Sound, Durants Island, Pamticoe Sound (Pamlico Sound), and Chichinock-cominock (Chicamacomico).

Killdevil Hills first showed up on a map in 1808, and a New Inlet appeared south of Bodie Island in the 1820s.

The derivation of these early place names is simple to trace. Many of them, including Roanoke, Hatteras, Croatan, Kitty Hawk, Kinnakeet, Currituck, Pamlico, and Chicamacomico came from Indian names. Several others, including Colington Island, Wimble Shoals, Manns Harbor, Bodie Island, and Durants Island, were the names of individuals associated with those places; while others, such as Alligator River, Stumpy Point, and New Inlet, were descriptive names used by early settlers to identify them.

Interesting legends are connected with the naming of Nags Head and Kill Devil Hills, both now incorporated resort towns on the Dare coast. More than a century ago a magazine writer stated that "Nag's Head derives its name, according to the prevalent etymology, from an old device employed to lure vessels to destruction. A Banks pony was driven up and down the beach at night, with a lantern tied around his neck. The up-and-down motion resembling that of a vessel, the unsuspecting tar would steer for it." Even earlier, however, the name was attributed to the contention that the Nags Head sand hills, from the sea, resembled the head of a horse resting on the flat sandy beach.

The name Kill Devil Hills is thought by many to have been bestowed on the area by the noted William Byrd of Virginia who in 1728 referred to the rum there as "so bad and unwholesome, that it is not improperly call'd 'Kill-Devil.'" Others tell the story of a man named Devil Ike who, when accused of stealing cargo from a wrecked ship blamed it on the devil; or another banker who was said to have consumated on top of Kill Devil Hills a deal whereby he traded his soul to the devil for a bag of gold and then tried to kill the devil.

A large proportion of the place names in Dare County, however, are of fairly recent origin, and as is the case throughout North Carolina the majority of these were bestowed by the United States Post Office Department. Only one post office, Hatteras, was in use when Dare County was formed in 1870, but others were established soon after.

A simple procedure was employed in establishing and naming a new post office at that time. It began with the request from some individual—usually a prominent merchant of a community —for postal service. He was then asked to provide information on the number of people who would be served and the nearest established post offices from which mail could be delivered; also he was asked to suggest three names for the proposed facility. If approved, the petitioner or a member of his family was usually named postmaster, and as often as not the new post office was located in his store or even in his home.

In this way three post offices, all named for Indians mentioned in the acounts of the Raleigh colonists, were soon established on Roanoke Island. The first, named Manteo, was opened in the county seat in 1873; the second, Wanchese, was established on the lower end of the island in 1886; and the third, Skyco, was established in 1892 at the steamer landing at Ashby's Harbor on the west side of the island, though this was later discontinued.

Hatteras Post Office had been established in 1858. A second, at Cape Hatteras, was authorized in 1873. Originally called The Cape, the name was changed to Buxton nine years later. Kinnakeet Post Office was established the same year, and it too was changed, to Avon, in 1883. Rodanthe was established at Chicamacomico in 1874, and Frisco at the community of Trent in 1898. Apparently the post office department refused to accept the name

Hatteras post office is shown here as it appeared in 1945. Photograph from the Travel and Promotion Division, State Department of Conservation and Development.

Chicamacomico because it was so hard to spell and pronounce, and it rejected Trent as a name because of possible confusion with the existing town of Trenton in Jones County. The other Hatteras Island post offices were Salvo, established at South Rodanthe in 1901, and Waves, which began operations in the old community of Clarks in 1939.

On the north banks, Kitty Hawk Post Office was established in 1876 and Nag's Head in 1884. A second post office in the Kitty Hawk area, Otila, was in existence briefly after 1905; and at one point the name of Nag's Head Post Office was changed to Griffin, then to Nag Head, and finally to Nags Head. Post offices, which are no longer in operation, were authorized for Colington in 1889 and Duck in 1909, and the Kill Devil Hills Post Office was established in 1938.

The first mainland post office was established at East Lake in 1875, quickly followed by those at Stumpy Point and Manns Harbor in 1876. Other mainland post offices, now no longer in existence, were Buffalo City, 1889; Mashoes, 1891; Juniper, 1903; Twiford, 1904; and Sycamore, 1906.

The Wright Brothers

Undoubtedly the little village of Kitty Hawk is known to more people throughout the world than is the state capital of Raleigh, or Charlotte, or any other place in North Carolina. For on the flat sands near the Kill Devil Hills just south of Kitty Hawk on December 17, 1903, Orville and Wilbur Wright of Dayton, Ohio, made the first successful flights in a motor-driven, heavier-than-air machine, and the age of human flight was born.

Today Kitty Hawk is an international aviation shrine marked by an impressive granite monument on top of the largest of the Kill Devil Hills and maintained by the National Park Service as the Wright Brothers National Memorial.

The Wright brothers became seriously interested in the problems of flight only four years before their success at Kitty Hawk. They were not trained scientists—neither of them even had a high school diploma—and they carried on their experiments in the time and with the money they could spare from the small bicycle business they operated in Dayton. For these reasons, and because they were in direct competition with some of the world's greatest scientists backed by large government appropriations and private contributions, many people have the impression that the accomplishments of the Wright brothers resulted more from luck than from ability and planning and work. They are wrong, for Orville and Wilbur Wright were among the greatest self-trained scientists the world has ever produced.

Wilbur was thirty-two years old and Orville twenty-seven when the older brother wrote to the Smithsonian Institution on May 30, 1899, for copies of all available papers and printed works on the subject of flight. "I believe," Wilbur said in that first letter, "that simple flight at least is possible to man and that experiments and investigations of a large number of independent workers will result in the accumulation of information and knowledge and skill which will finally lead to accomplished flight." He then added, "I wish to avail myself of all that is already known and then if possible add my mite to help on the future worker who will attain final success."

A careful study of the material sent them by the Smithsonian convinced the brothers that the failure of earlier experiments—which had caused the death of at least two scientists—resulted from their inability to balance their machines properly in the air. Since "these experimenters had attempted to maintain balance merely by the shifting of the weight of their bodies," Orville said later, "we at once set to work to devise a more efficient means of maintaining the equilibrium." Their conclusion, after less than two months of study, was that the answer was to make the wings flexible so they could be warped in flight.

That winter they built a glider large enough to carry a man, and by the summer of 1900 they were ready to begin actual experiments. For this purpose they sought a place where they could be off by themselves and where they could find steady winds and flat terrain with nearby steep hills for gliding.

Data secured from the United States Weather Bureau indicated that Kitty Hawk on the North Carolina Outer Banks was one of several places which might suit their needs, and after corresponding with Joseph J. Dosher of the weather bureau station at Kitty Hawk and former postmaster William J. Tate, they made plans to take their glider to Kitty Hawk in the fall.

Wilbur arrived at Kitty Hawk on September 13, 1900, and pitched a tent on a hill overlooking Kitty Hawk Bay. Orville followed several days later with the glider and additional supplies. They remained for five weeks, flying their glider as a kite in winds up to thirty miles per hour and keeping accurate records of their experiments, making slight alterations to the machine and perfecting their ability to control it.

Back in Dayton that winter they analyzed the data they obtained and then constructed a larger and much improved glider, with which they returned again to Kitty Hawk for experiments in the summer of 1901. This time they moved down the beach to the base of the largest of the sand hills known as the Kill Devil Hills and built a sixteen by twenty-five foot building in which to live and work on their machine. They made hundreds of tests with their new glider, often with a man on board, and on one particular gliding flight of 335 feet established what was thought to be a world record.

For four successive years, from 1900 through 1903, Orville and Wilbur Wright continued this procedure, experimenting at Kitty Hawk in the summer and fall, then analyzing their data and building a new, larger and improved machine back at Dayton in the winter and spring. They found that much of the information accumulated by others experimenting with flight was incorrect, and in almost every area they studied the mistakes of others, then conducted their own experiments and devised their own methods of correcting the errors.

In this manner they compiled the first accurate detailed charts on wind resistance, built the first wind tunnel in which different types of wing surfaces were actually tested, designed and built a motor for their flying machine which was lighter and more efficient than any before produced by engineers, and developed propellers especially suited for their needs.

In the process they made more than one thousand gliding flights at Kitty Hawk in 1902 and broke all existing records for distance and time in flight. When they returned to the Outer Banks in the fall of 1903 they had progressed to the stage where they were ready to attempt to fly in a motor-driven machine capable of lifting off from flat ground with a human being at the controls and rising into the air for sustained flight.

They reached Kitty Hawk in late September, 1903, and practiced with their 1902 glider while getting ready for the first attempt at powered flight. For nearly two months they suffered one setback after another—storms, malfunctioning parts, and a

In this photograph of the Wright brothers' first flight at Kitty Hawk on December 17, 1903, Wilbur is shown at the right of the picture beside the airplane and Orville is at the controls. Department of Archives and History photograph.

Orville Wright, standing behind the stooping boy on the left, attended the dedication of the Wright Memorial at Kitty Hawk on November 19, 1932. Photograph from the National Archives.

propeller which broke loose, necessitating two trips to Dayton for repairs—but by December 11 they were ready for the final test. Unfortunately, wind conditions were not proper until the morning of December 17, but when Orville mounted the machine for the first test at 10:30 A.M., started the motor, and rolled forward with Wilbur running beside steadying the wings, conditions were right at last.

Orville's first history-making flight covered only about one hundred feet and lasted twelve seconds. Wilbur then took his turn, flying for a longer period of time and a greater distance, then Orville again, and finally Wilbur for a fourth flight which lasted fifty-seven seconds and covered a distance of 852 feet.

Thus, on the isolated North Carolina Outer Banks, two young bicycle makers from Ohio, untrained as scientists yet possessing intelligence, a willingness to work, and the faculty for systematically analyzing their findings, ushered in the modern era of human flight. Today a full-scale reproduction of their original flying machine plus numerous other exhibits which combine to tell the story of their success are on display in the visitor center at the Wright Memorial.

Commercial Fisheries

Though seafood has always been a staple in the Outer Banks diet and the first recorded instance of profit from a business activity on the coast was the extraction of oil from dead whales by the settlers at Colington in the 1660s, there is a widely believed but false impression that fishing has always been the backbone of the area's economy.

In actual fact commercial fishing was of primary importance as a source of income on the Outer Banks for only a relatively brief period beginning after the Civil War and ending with World War II. Prior to the 1870s the great difficulty in getting fresh fish to market without refrigeration was an overwhelming deterrent to development of the fisheries, and since the 1940s tourism has emerged as the leading industry in Dare County.

Even the term "commercial fisheries" is misleading, for some of the most successful ventures in this category have involved products of the sea other than fish, most notably whales and porpoises (mammals), turtles and terrapins (reptiles), oysters and clams (mollusks), shrimp and crabs (crustaceans), and even seaweed (plants).

During the colonial period and the early years of statehood many dead whales washed up on the beach, and a number of

Women and young men of an Outer Banks community make fishing nets around 1899. Photograph from the collection of Collier Cobb, courtesy of Miss Mary Cobb.

Fishermen crate fish at the Stumpy Point fishery around 1945. Photograph from the Travel and Promotion Division, State Department of Conservation and Development.

people derived their principle income by cutting off huge chunks of blubber and boiling it to remove the whale oil. Residents also sold baleen, commonly known as whalebone, a horny substance growing inside the whale's mouth and used by the giant mammals as food strainers.

The first extensive efforts to harvest a commercial crop from the coastal waters of North Carolina involved those species of fish which could be preserved by salting without losing their commercial value. Thus the earliest really successful commercial fishing ventures were the mullet fisheries in the shallow waters back of the Outer Banks and the herring and shad fisheries in the sounds and rivers.

For many years the big cash crop for Dare County fishermen was shad, a bony but much sought after food fish which spends a large part of its life at sea but which must spawn in fresh water. Each spring huge schools of shad pass through the inlets of the Outer Banks heading toward their principal spawning grounds in Albemarle Sound and its tributaries. The Dare County fishermen, particularly on Roanoke Island and the mainland communities of Stumpy Point, Manns Harbor, and Mashoes, learned to catch the shad by stretching their nets between poles imbedded in the sandy bottom of the shallow sounds in such a manner as to funnel the fish into their nets and thus impound them. These were known as "pound nets" and were so extensive in the Croatan Sound area that they became "almost complete barriers to the passage of the fish," resulting in a 1905 law "maintaining an open channel, free from nets of all kinds, from the inlets to the spawning grounds."

A particular delicacy in northern markets was shad roe, found in large sacs in female shad enroute to the spawning grounds. Since this roe was actually shad eggs, the early lack of restrictions on catching "roe shad" was a primary factor in the decline of the important shad fisheries, and in recent years shad fishing has been of relatively minor importance in Dare County.

Among the other fisheries which figured prominently in the early development of the industry in the Outer Banks area were those which involved porpoise and terrapin, both of which were "fished out" in a relatively short period of time, and oysters, which remained for years as a major commercial fishing product.

Diamondback terrapins, first cousins to turtles, average not more than six inches in length when full grown and were once in great demand for terrapin soup and terrapin stew. The first effort to catch them commercially in the area was made at Bodie Island in 1849, and one man that year received $750 for more than four thousand diamondbacks. As is so typical in the coastal fisheries, others immediately got in on the act and within a few years the supply was so diminished that the price rose to an average of more than $30 per dozen, and as the creatures became nearly extinct sales were recorded as high as $120 per dozen.

The porpoise or dolphin, a mammal know to every schoolchild by the exploits of Flipper, was valued primarily for its oil, and for a brief period in the 1880s a porpoise factory was in operation at Hatteras. Several crews using heavy nets fished the Hatteras beach for porpoise in order to keep the factory going, and in one six-month period a single crew caught nearly thirteen hundred of these graceful and intelligent mammals.

Oysters require a certain degree of salinity in the water in order to grow properly, and thus they are found in great beds— known in early times as "oyster rocks"—most often located in proximity to inlets. At one time their primary commercial use was as fertilizer, but later they were harvested extensively for table use. For many years individual fishermen have been allowed to claim private oyster beds by registering them with the local clerk of court, a practice still in effect, though there has been considerable controversy over these rights. About 1890 the large oyster beds in Chesapeake Bay were practically fished out, and the Chesapeake oystermen invaded the North Carolina sounds with armed boats, removing large quantities of North Carolina oysters to restock their Virginia and Maryland beds.

Other products of the commercial fisheries through the years have been clams, sturgeon (large ocean fish valued especially for their eggs and caught briefly along the Outer Banks in the early part of this century), menhaden (small, oily school fish usually processed into fertilizer or animal food), croakers, bluefish, spot, and striped bass or rock.

Shrimp were long considered of no commercial value and when caught in fishnets were thrown overboard, but when North Carolina's commercial fishermen realized the growing extent of the nation's appetite for shrimp as a table food they went all out in their efforts to harvest the crop, and for a brief time after

Fishermen clean and paint a fishing boat at the Hatteras docks in 1948. Photograph from the Travel and Promotion Division, State Department of Conservation and Development.

World War II shrimp was the big money crop for the fishermen in the sounds. As was the case with so many other varieties, however, the combination of overfishing, lack of concern for reasonable conservation practices, and pollution has reduced the shrimp fishery to a minor role.

Traditionally the commercial fishing activities in Dare County have been small boat operations, frequently involving only one and at most no more than three or four men. In those cases where crews fished long nets in the sound or haul nets from the ocean beach, they operated on a share basis, with the expenses being deducted first from the proceeds and the rest divided with one or more shares going to the owner of the rig and single shares to each man in the crew.

As in so many other occupations it has become increasingly difficult for the small operator to make a living from commercial fishing, and in recent years there has been a trend toward larger operations. Wanchese, on the lower end of Roanoke Island and closest port to Oregon Inlet, has become the center for larger

Fishermen pull haul nets from the surf at Hatteras. Photograph from the Travel and Promotion Division, State Department of Conservation and Development.

trawl boat operations, and Wanchese boats now operate on occasion as far away as the New England coast in search of almost anything they can catch, including scallops, flounder, and swordfish.

Ironically, as this is written, the product of the coastal fisheries producing the largest annual tonnage and the greatest cash income is not fish but crabs, and in Dare County today it is probable that more commercial fishermen are engaged in crabbing than in all other commercial fishing activities combined. Crabbing is still basically a small boat operation, often carried on by a single man who leaves his dock well before dawn in the warmer months to "fish" his crab pots. Later in the day when he sorts out his catch he removes the "peelers" and places them in a specially designed sunken box where the peelers shed and become soft crabs, a much more valuable commodity than are the hard crabs.

Some few others concentrate on soft crabbing, wading the shallow waters along the sound shore in search of blue crabs which have already shed their hard shells. But many fishermen engage in crabbing only on a part-time basis and are employed in the construction trades in the resort areas for the rest of the year.

What about the seaweed mentioned earlier as a product of our commercial fisheries? Well, shortly before the outbreak of the First World War a number of people at Avon regularly gathered eel grass which had washed ashore on the sound side of the banks, carefully dried and baled it, and shipped it off to Baltimore and High Point and other markets where it was used in making mattresses and in stuffing furniture. Despite the advent of foam rubber they might still be doing it, too, except that a blight killed off the eel grass in Pamlico Sound in the 1920s.

Religion and Education

Religious activity on the Outer Banks has always been more than just going to church on Sunday, reading the Bible in the evening, and saying grace before meals.

Until comparatively recently the absence of theaters, auditoriums, and parks made the church and its grounds the center for civic and social activities, and with no formal educational facilities in the isolated banks' communities the preacher often had to double as a teacher.

Though Dare County was the scene of the first recorded Protestant religious ceremony in this hemisphere when the Indian Manteo was baptized on August 13, 1587, on Roanoke Island, there is little mention of religious affairs for the ensuing two hundred and fifty years.

Apparently the first minister to settle in the area was a man named James Adams, who was sent to the colony in 1708 by the Society for the Propagation of the Gospel and lived briefly in Currituck. He brought with him from England one of the first libraries established in North Carolina and left his collection of books to the people of Currituck, though there is no record of what happened to them. In all probability he also conducted the first school sessions in the area, since this was considered one of the objectives of those sent to the colonies by the society.

James Gamewell, a "Minister of the Gospel," purchased a homesite in the vicinity of Kitty Hawk in 1783, but it was not until the Civil War that there appeared written evidence of the

The church at Mashoes is shown here as it appeared in 1942. Photograph from the Travel and Promotion Division, State Department of Conservation and Development.

existence of church buildings in most of the Outer Banks communities.

Most of the early churches were Baptist, Methodist, and Pentecostal—and most still are for that matter—though an Episcopal church has been located at Nags Head for a number of years, a Catholic church was established at Kill Devil Hills in the 1930s, and in recent years other denominations have been conducting summer services in the beach areas.

The shortage of trained theologians for service in the small Outer Banks churches resulted many years ago in a system whereby a single minister was responsible for a "charge" of several churches, preaching in different communities on alternate Sundays, or where visiting preachers conducted services once a month or so. This did not mean that the church buildings were locked up on those Sundays when there was no minister in attendance, for almost all of the denominations serving the coast conducted regular weekly services with lay preachers or lay readers.

In times past the big religious affairs were the camp meetings or revivals usually held once or twice a year when the Methodists or Baptists from all of the Outer Banks communities converged on a single church for a full day, or sometimes two or three days, of religious and social activities. Preaching, singing, and prayer meetings were the basis for the religious phases of these extensive gatherings, but just as important were the "grub on the ground" meals, for which the women of the parish would cook great quantities of food, sometimes drafting the men to help with a big fish fry.

Even today hardly a month passes when some church in Dare County doesn't put on a big fish fry or chicken dinner, though more often than not these meals are sponsored more as a means of raising funds than as religious gatherings or social get-togethers. Individual churches are involved also in the sponsorship of Boy Scout and Girl Scout units and in other youth activities, and beginning in 1968 the Dare County Ministerial Association sponsored the highly successful summer Circus Tent at Kill Devil Hills, which featured four programs of folk singing nightly by the New Hermeneutics, combined with an ice cream parlor manned by volunteer crews.

Prior to the beginning of this century formal education was limited to occasional efforts at teaching classes by ministers, or private tutoring. Then most communities began to import teachers who would come in for three or four months at the time, teaching their classes first in private homes or churches and later in small wooden schoolhouses. More regular school sessions were established in most sections of the county after the First World War, and free public schools for all children became a reality when the state took over the basic educational system in the 1930s.

As in so many other areas of Outer Banks life, the difficulties involved in arranging transportation between communities resulted in the necessity of having small schools in each community. Then the construction of roads and bridges and a state-wide move toward consolidation resulted in the closing of many of the smaller schools in the 1950s.

New consolidated schools have been built in recent years to serve all of the children, and today there are three elementary schools in the county—at Manteo, Cape Hatteras, and Kitty Hawk—and two high schools—at Manteo and Buxton. For the

This modern high school was built at Manteo about 1960. Photograph by Aycock Brown.

most part the Negro population of Dare County has been centered on Roanoke Island, and in the mid-1960s the Dare County schools were fully integrated.

As for recreational activities, there are two moving picture theaters in the county, at Manteo and Avon, and the resort area on the Dare beaches provides a variety of entertainment ranging from dance halls to amusement centers.

An application has been filed recently for construction of a radio station on Roanoke Island, and most residents of the county get relatively good television and radio reception from stations in Norfolk, Virginia, and on the mainland of North Carolina.

In the 1930s a Dare County native, D. Victor Meekins, having gained experience as a newspaper reporter on papers in other sections, returned to Manteo and began publication of the *Dare County Times*, still being published by his family as the *Coastland Times*. Seasonal publications, the *Surfside News* at Kill Devil Hills and *Hatteras Island Breakers* at Buxton, are provided for the tourists coming into the area.

On the cultural side, a number of art galleries have been established on Roanoke Island and the beaches, and art classes and exhibitions are regular features of the summer season. The Dare County Chapter of the North Carolina Symphony Society began sponsoring visits by the North Carolina Symphony Orchestra in 1969 for free performances for all Dare County schoolchildren.

Of all their accomplishments, however, many residents of Dare County are most proud of their new, modern library in Manteo. The outgrowth of a Woman's Club project many years ago, the library was expanded under county sponsorship to include countywide bookmobile service, and it is now considered one of the finest small county public libraries in the state.

Roads and Bridges

For nearly three and a half centuries after discovery of the area by the Raleigh colonists, the course of life on the Outer Banks was dictated by its inaccessibility. Small boats were the accepted mode of transportation between Hatteras Island, the north banks, Roanoke Island, and the mainland, and the people were so accustomed to moving about on the water that many of them would prefer to pole a skiff half a mile down the shore to visit a neighbor rather than walk on the sandy trails.

The catch of fresh fish, amounting to many thousands of hundred-pound boxes annually, had to be transported to Elizabeth City or Norfolk by boat; all supplies had to be brought in by boat; and when people left the area, even when there were emergency medical conditions, the only recourse was to travel by boat.

This inaccessibility and limited contact with the rest of North Carolina—and with the rest of the world too, for that matter—inevitably resulted in residents of the Outer Banks retaining the habits, speech, and daily practices of their forbears, as described in the earlier chapter dealing with "Early Life on the Outer Banks." Theirs was a slow pace, considered backward by outsiders accustomed to the increased tempo and pressure of modern society and technological development, yet it was a way of life which rested on a solid foundation of self-sufficiency, belief in the Almighty, and independence.

Though the inaccessibility retarded development and economic growth, many Dare County people liked things the way they were and wanted to keep them that way. But even the strong-willed Outer Bankers could not resist the intrusion of "modern improvements" forever.

Power boats came first, then automobiles, and it is said at

Wooden tracks such as those pictured here were employed to get cars over the dunes of the Outer Banks before the advent of hard-surfaced roads. Photograph from Bill Sharpe, *A New Geography of North Carolina*, I, 80.

Buxton that the first two cars on the island, traveling the wide flat beach at low tide in opposite directions, had a head-on collision. Even without interference from other vehicles, however, driving on the beach or the sandy trails was a tricky business involving properly deflating the tires, experience in staying in the tracks of the last car which had passed that way, and work for strong backs when the car got stuck.

Hard-surfaced roads were the obvious answer to this problem, and the first one was built by the county on Roanoke Island in the 1920s, but there was no need for anything resembling a network of modern highways so long as the motorist's trip was limited by the length of the particular island on which he was driving.

There was talk in the 1920s of a road down the beach from Kitty Hawk to Nags Head and bridges to connect the north banks with the mainland and with Roanoke Island, but highway engineers questioned whether a highway could be built and maintained on the exposed sandy beach, and the administrators controlling state highway funds could see no economic justification for major expenditures in the remote coastal area.

It was at this point, in 1927, that the Dare County Board of Commissioners, prodded by Chairman Washington Baum, took matters into their own hands by floating a bond issue and contracting for construction of a toll bridge from Roanoke Island to Nags Head. Shortly afterward a group of Elizabeth City businessmen who owned extensive beach property at Kitty Hawk made plans for constructing a second toll bridge, this one across Currituck Sound from Point Harbor to Kitty Hawk.

Meanwhile Dare County borrowed more money to build dirt roads through the mainland swamps to connect Manns Harbor with Stumpy Point and East Lake. Private citizens from Kitty Hawk, Colington, and Wanchese began operating small ferries— at first consisting of nothing more than flat barges towed by motor boats and large enough for only one or two cars—across Oregon Inlet to connect with Hatteras Island and across Croatan Sound and Alligator River to connect with the mainland communities to the west.

When the two bridges, the first more than a mile long and the second nearly three miles long, were completed, the state at long last had no choice but to connect them with an asphalt surfaced road down the north banks. Later the state took over the Roanoke Sound bridge from the county, purchased the bridge over Curri-

The Oregon Inlet ferry, shown here in 1946, operated between Hatteras Island and Bodie Island. Photograph from the Travel and Promotion Division, State Department of Conservation and Development.

Today the modern Herbert C. Bonner Bridge spans Oregon Inlet to connect the two islands. Photograph by Aycock Brown.

tuck Sound from the Wright Memorial Bridge Company, and made both toll-free. Still later, after World War II, the state purchased the private ferries and removed the tolls and finally built modern bridges across Croatan Sound in 1953, Alligator River in 1959, and Oregon Inlet in 1963, replaced the original Roanoke Sound and Currituck Sound bridges with wider and more modern structures, hard-surfaced the roads on the mainland, and built a modern highway from Oregon Inlet to Hatteras.

It took local initiative and daring and private investment to begin the long and costly process of making the Outer Banks accessible at last, but today there are five beautiful modern bridges in or connecting with Dare County, averaging more than two miles each in length, and they in turn are joined by a network of modern roads in all parts of the county.

Tourism

One of the few successful outside intrusions on the complacent life of the Outer Banks was the development of Nags Head into a full-fledged seaside resort or "watering place" beginning in the 1830s. Even then the changes which resulted were more evident among the visitors to the resort than to the natives, for it was accepted practice for the tourists to slip into the easygoing pace of Outer Banks life.

The most obvious evidences of this transformation from outlander to banker, which seemed to affect the visitor almost automatically the very moment he set foot on the old wooden dock on the Nags Head soundside, were the casting aside of the inhibitions of mainland society, turning the children free to play or fish or loaf as they saw fit, spending the day in old clothes or near the water, and going barefoot to the nightly square dances.

Nags Head was a family resort, informal and easygoing, frequented for the most part by families from Elizabeth City, Hertford, and Edenton whose women and children spent the summer there from early June to Labor Day and were joined on weekends by the planter, lawyer, or businessman father. Even to this day, with the resort area spreading out as far as Hatteras, Roanoke Island, and Duck, the appeal of the Dare coast resort area remains the same. People still vacation there because of the informality, the slow pace, and the wide open spaces.

The first hotel at Nags Head was built near the soundside soon after the annual migration of summer visitors began, and long before the outbreak of the Civil War there was a hotel larger than any now located on the coast, with a ballroom, bar, bowling alley, dining room, and covered porches on all sides. By the 1850s a dock had been constructed half a mile out into Roanoke Sound to accommodate the little packet schooners and side-wheel steamboats which transported the visitors, and a railway boasting a single horse-pulled car ran from the dock across the dunes to the seaside.

Many of the regular visitors built summer cottages along the sound shore, though it was not an infrequent occurrence for these to be covered over by the sand blowing across the bare banks from the beach. In this manner also a large hotel gradually disappeared in the period following the Civil War.

Early Nags Head visitors invariably climbed the highest of the sand hills in the area, Jockey's Ridge, just as do the tourists of today. Though the cool prevailing breezes coming off the sound and the easy access to the calm sound waters for sailing,

Jockey's Ridge, the largest of the sand dunes at Nag's Head, is a popular attraction for tourists to the area. Photograph from the Travel and Promotion Division, State Department of Conservation and Development.

56

crabbing, fishing, and swimming had resulted in the location of the early resort on the Nags Head soundside, by the turn of the century the newer visitors were beginning to build their cottages nearer the ocean.

The resort area was confined to a stretch immediately south of Jockey's Ridge and extending north and south for approximately a mile until access by automobile was provided by the construction of the bridges and roads in the late 1920s and early 1930s. Thereafter the resort development began to spread southward toward Bodie Island and eventually to Hatteras and Buxton and north past Kill Devil Hills to Kitty Hawk and Southern Shores. The opening of Paul Green's symphonic drama *The Lost Colony* in the Waterside Theater at Fort Raleigh in the summer of 1937, now the longest running outdoor historical drama in America, brought Roanoke Island into the act, and many private homes began to take in summer tourists there.

Today there are more modern motel and hotel rooms, more rental cottages, more public and private campsites in Dare County than at any other oceanfront resort area on the North Carolina coast, and the original mile-long Nags Head resort now covers nearly seventy-five miles of oceanfront beach and many more miles on the sounds.

Large charter boat fleets now operate out of Oregon Inlet and Hatteras, and the latter community is host to an annual Blue Marlin Fishing Tournament and bills itself as the "Blue Marlin Capital of the World." Annual surf-fishing tournaments are held at Nags Head and Buxton, while Kitty Hawk Bay and Currituck

Modern motels such as the one shown here offer accommodations for visitors to the Dare coast. Photograph by Aycock Brown.

Charter boats docked at the Oregon Inlet Fishing Center are available to enthusiasts of deep-sea fishing. Photograph by Aycock Brown.

Sound and their tributaries are renowned for their bass fishing, and the operators of small rental boats out of Wanchese are so confident that anybody can catch something in the nearby sounds that they guarantee you will catch fish or there will be no charge for using the boat.

Skin diving has become a popular sport, particularly in the vicinity of offshore wrecks, and more and more surfers are being drawn to the Dare coast area each year. Numerous launching ramps in the area make it possible for the sailing or water-skiing enthusiast to choose a wide variety of different bodies of inland water in Dare County, and those not so ambitious are attracted by the opportunities for swimming, shelling, and bird watching. As a final touch, two golf courses have been constructed in the Kitty Hawk area.

Unfortunately, except in isolated instances, the resort property has been developed independently by owners of small parcels of land, with little thought for future planning and for retaining natural attractions and public use areas. However, an active planning program by the county government and zoning controls by the recently created municipalities of Nags Head and Kill Devil Hills, plus more farsighted planning by some of the larger private developers, has started a trend toward long-range planning with the ultimate goal of retaining as much as possible the natural beauty and informality of the area while at the same time providing modern facilities for the tourists.

National Park Facilities

In the relatively brief period of time since resort development on the Dare Coast began expanding beyond the original one mile of beach at old Nags Head, a stretch of oceanfrontage approximately twenty-five miles in length has been heavily developed and is now lined almost solidly with private cottages, motels, and resort businesses.

At the current accelerated pace of development all of the once open and isolated Dare ocean shoreline would be converted into privately owned building sites within a few years, thus cutting off forever access to this majestic creation of nature for all except the few who owned property there; and even then, the beach would bear little resemblance to the Outer Banks of old.

Fortunately this will never happen, for more than half of the oceanfront beach in Dare County, forty-odd miles of it, is included within the confines of the nation's first national seashore recreational area, to remain forever in its natural state, yet accessible to each man, woman, and child of every future generation.

Within the borders of the Cape Hatteras National Seashore today are both the Cape Hatteras lighthouse and the Bodie Island lighthouse; the old Chicamacomico, Little Kinnakeet, and Bodie Island Coast Guard stations; the Pea Island National Wildlife Refuge; Cape Hatteras; the buried remnants of dozens of old shipwrecks; and a continuous stretch of Outer Banks beach extending from the south end of Nags Head the length of Hatteras Island to Hatteras Inlet.

Authorization to establish this National Park Service facility was granted by Congress during the depression of the 1930s, and thousands of Works Projects Administration (WPA) laborers and Civilian Conservation Corps (CCC) boys were engaged for several years in a major effort to build up the low beaches and control erosion by erecting sand fences and planting grass. A provision of the act establishing the National Seashore was that all lands had to be donated, and the nucleus of the park, the point at Cape Hatteras, was donated by the John S. and Henry Phipps families, owners of two gunning clubs in the vicinity of Buxton and Avon.

With the approach of World War II the dune restoration, grass planting, and erosion control projects were halted. Shortly afterward oil companies began drilling in the area, and though they appear to have drilled some of the deepest wells ever attempted up to that time without striking oil, their actions served to increase interest in the possibilities of private development of the Hatteras Island beaches.

When the movement to continue with acquisition of land for the park was resumed after the war there was strong opposition from some of the property owners, but when the Old Dominion and Avalon foundations—both established by the Mellon family— offered to match funds with the state of North Carolina for acquisition of the remaining land needed, the Cape Hatteras National Seashore Recreational Area was finally assured.

Even before this, beginning in 1929, Kill Devil Hill, scene of the Wright brothers' gliding experiments, had been stabilized with native woods mold and grasses. Construction of the Wright Memorial monument on top of the hill was completed in 1932, and the following year the facility became a national monument

An aerial view shows the Waterside Theater, setting for the outdoor drama *The Lost Colony*, at the Fort Raleigh National Historic Site on Roanoke Island. Photograph by Aycock Brown.

under jurisdiction of the National Park Service. Not long after that the Fort Raleigh National Historic Site was established on Roanoke Island.

Today more than a third of the National Park Service facilities in North Carolina are located in Dare County, with both the Wright Brothers National Monument at Kill Devil Hills and the Fort Raleigh National Historic Site on Roanoke Island being administered by the superintendent of the larger Cape Hatteras National Seashore Recreational Area.

In addition to seeing the reconstructed earthworks at Fort Raleigh, inspecting the actual site of man's first flight in a heavier-than-air machine at Kill Devil Hill, and walking the miles of uncrowded beaches of the Cape Hatteras National Seashore, the visitor to Dare County now has a wide choice of visitor centers, museums, nature trails, and other Park Service facilities from which to choose. These include the Museum of the Sea adjacent to the Cape Hatteras lighthouse; the lighthouse itself,

Sun shelters and bathhouses are convenient for use by visitors to the Coquina Beach day-use facility on Bodie Island. Photograph by Aycock Brown.

which is open to the public; the natural history museum at the Bodie Island lighthouse; Coquina Beach day-use facility, including picnic areas and bathing beaches, on Bodie Island; the visitor center and reconstructed Wright plane, hanger, and workshop at the Wright Memorial; the visitor center at the Lost Colony theater and the area Park Service headquarters at Fort Raleigh; and large campgrounds at Oregon Inlet, Salvo, Cape Hatteras, and Frisco.

Conclusion

The Raleigh colonists described the Outer Banks as "the goodliest land under the cope of heav'n."

Orville Wright complained that mosquitoes attacked him in "vast multitudes" resulting in "the most miserable existence I had ever passed through."

The truth lies somewhere in between, for the Dare Coast was neither so good nor so bad as these famous visitors claimed. It still isn't, though in recent years man has partially defiled the land about which Raleigh's men wrote in such glowing terms, and he has partially controlled the mosquitoes about which Orville Wright complained so forcefully.

There is so much of historical significance in this land of broad shallow sounds and low sandy islands that much of it is overlooked or is so taken for granted by the residents as to be ignored.

Where else would the experiments of Reginald Fessenden—conducted between Roanoke Island and Hatteras in 1901 and resulting in the first successful wireless telegraphy transmission over such a distance—be treated so lightly as to take up only a sentence in the conclusion of a book? Where else could people live within sight of the spot where in all probability the first English flag was planted in America, yet have no knowledge of it and no evident concern over its significance? And where else could people live in such close proximity to the birthplace of modern aviation as to be almost entirely unconcerned over the annual pilgrimage there of the world's aviation leaders?

There are so many facets of Outer Banks history for which there is no space for details in a brief summary of this kind. Yet there is as much romance and color in the accounts of the annual wild pony pennings on the Outer Banks in earlier times as there is in any story of roundup days in the old West, and there was enough excitement in the fabulous duck, goose, and brant hunting which took place on the Dare Coast in the days before the bridges to satisfy any of the sportsmen who came from all parts of the world to test their gunning skill.

A chapter could be written on the successful efforts of the Roanoke Island Historical Association, and its predecessors, to preserve the Fort Raleigh site on Roanoke Island and later to sponsor *The Lost Colony* drama for a run of more than thirty years; or on the dream of leaders of the North Carolina Association of Garden Clubs to establish an Elizabethan Garden adjacent to the site of the Roanoke colonization attempts, now a beautiful reality.

No apologies are made for omissions in this brief history of Dare County, for it is intended to answer the questions most often asked about the area. At the same time, though, it attempts to convey something of the feel of these long-isolated and lonely islands extending seaward off the North Carolina coast, and if you have read this far, then perhaps this mission was accomplished.

An Apollo 9 spacecraft view taken in March, 1969, shows the North Carolina coast. Cape Hatteras juts farthest into the Atlantic, with Cape Lookout below it. Photograph from the National Aeronautics and Space Administration, loaned by the North Carolina Citizens Association, Inc.

ADDITIONAL READING

Barrett, John Gilchrist. *North Carolina as a Civil War Battleground, 1861–1865*. Raleigh: Division of Archives and History, North Carolina Department of Cultural Resources, eleventh printing, 1995.

Bishir, Catherine W. *The "Unpainted Aristocracy": The Beach Cottages of Old Nags Head*. Raleigh: Division of Archives and History, North Carolina Department of Cultural Resources, third printing, 1983 [originally published as an article in the *North Carolina Historical Review* 54 (October 1977): 367–392].

Ellis, William S. "Lonely Cape Hatteras, Besieged by the Sea." *National Geographic* 136 (September 1969): 393–421.

Mobley, Joe A. *Ship Ashore! The U.S. Lifesavers of Coastal North Carolina*. Raleigh: Division of Archives and History, North Carolina Department of Cultural Resources, 1994.

Parramore, Thomas C. *Triumph at Kitty Hawk: The Wright Brothers and Powered Flight*. Raleigh: Division of Archives and History, North Carolina Department of Cultural Resources, 1993.

Powell, William S. *Paradise Preserved*. Chapel Hill: University of North Carolina Press, 1965.

Rankin, Hugh F. *The Pirates of Colonial North Carolina*. Raleigh: Division of Archives and History, North Carolina Department of Cultural Resources, eighteenth printing, 1994.

Sharpe, Bill. "Dare [County]." *A New Geography of North Carolina*, vol. 1. Raleigh: Sharpe Publishing Company, 1954, pp. 73–114.

Stick, David. *Graveyard of the Atlantic*. Chapel Hill: University of North Carolina Press, 1952.

———. *North Carolina Lighthouses*. Raleigh: Division of Archives and History, North Carolina Department of Cultural Resources, twelfth printing, 1995.

———. *The Outer Banks of North Carolina, 1584–1958*. Chapel Hill: University of North Carolina Press, 1958.

———. *Roanoke Island: The Beginnings of English America*. Chapel Hill: University of North Carolina Press for America's Four Hundredth Anniversary Committee, 1983.

Stick, David, and Bruce Roberts. *The Cape Hatteras Seashore*. Charlotte: McNally and Loftin, 1964.